GEORGIA BULLDOGS

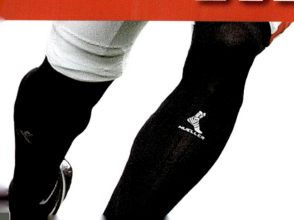

LUKE HANLON

Apex is distributed by North Star Editions:
sales@northstareditions.com | 888-417-0195

Produced for Apex by Red Line Editorial.

Photographs ©: Brian Rothmuller/Icon Sportswire/AP Images, cover, 1; James Gilbert/Getty Images Sport/Getty Images, 4–5; David J. Griffin/Icon Sportswire/AP Images, 6–7, 58–59; Shutterstock Images, 8–9; George Rinhart/Corbis Historical/Getty Images, 10–11; Bettmann/Getty Images, 12–13, 14–15, 20–21; Gene Blythe/AP Images, 16–17; AP Images, 19, 24–25, 26–27; REJ/AP Images, 22–23; Al Messerschmidt/AP Images, 29, 57; Allen Dean Steele/Allsport/Getty Images Sport/Getty Images, 30–31; Matthew Stockman/Getty Images Sport/Getty Images, 32–33; Scott Cunningham/Getty Images Sport/Getty Images, 34–35, 42–43; Jamie Schwaberow/Getty Images Sport/Getty Images, 36–37; Andy Lyons/Allsport/ Getty Images Sport/Getty Images, 38–39; Kevin C. Cox/Getty Images Sport/Getty Images, 40–41, 44–45; Adam Hagy/Getty Images Sport/Getty Images, 47; Brandon Sloter/Image Of Sport/Getty Images Sport/Getty Images, 48–49; Carmen Mandato/Getty Images Sport/Getty Images, 50–51; Butch Dill/Getty Images Sport/Getty Images, 52–53; Austin McAfee/Icon Sportswire/AP Images, 54–55

Library of Congress Control Number: 2025930330

ISBN
979-8-89250-711-0 (hardcover)
979-8-89250-763-9 (paperback)
979-8-89250-746-2 (ebook pdf)
979-8-89250-729-5 (hosted ebook)

Printed in the United States of America
Mankato, MN
082025

NOTE TO PARENTS AND EDUCATORS

Apex books are designed to build literacy skills in striving readers. Exciting, high-interest content attracts and holds readers' attention. The text is carefully leveled to allow students to achieve success quickly.

TABLE OF CONTENTS

CHAPTER 1

GO DAWGS!

More than 93,000 fans pack Sanford Stadium. They all point to a trumpeter in the stands. That band member starts playing the "Battle Hymn of Bulldog Nation." Soon, the whole band joins in.

Georgia's marching band is known as the Redcoats.

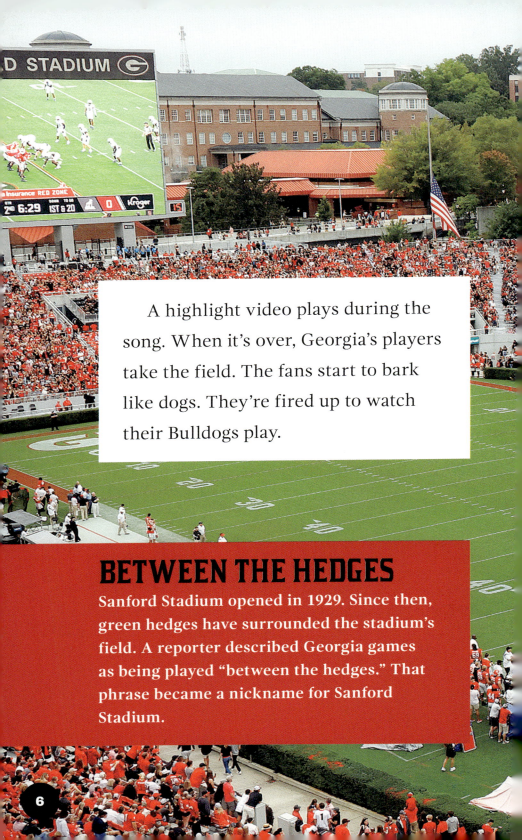

A highlight video plays during the song. When it's over, Georgia's players take the field. The fans start to bark like dogs. They're fired up to watch their Bulldogs play.

BETWEEN THE HEDGES

Sanford Stadium opened in 1929. Since then, green hedges have surrounded the stadium's field. A reporter described Georgia games as being played "between the hedges." That phrase became a nickname for Sanford Stadium.

Georgia fans dress in red for Bulldogs football games.

CHAPTER 2

EARLY HISTORY

The University of Georgia opened in 1785. The school is in Athens, Georgia. In 1892, Charles Holmes Herty formed the school's football team. That January, Georgia won its first game. The team beat Mercer College 50–0.

ROBERT E. PARK HALL

The University of Georgia is one of the oldest public universities in the United States.

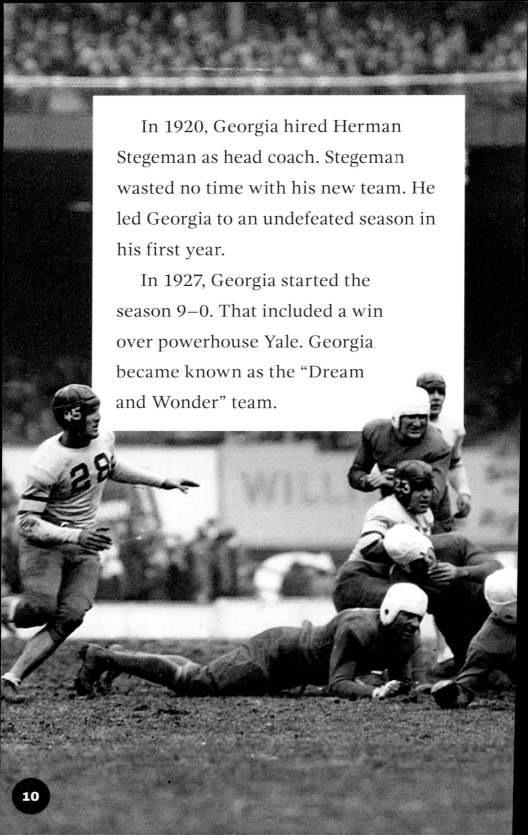

In 1920, Georgia hired Herman
Stegeman as head coach. Stegeman
wasted no time with his new team. He
led Georgia to an undefeated season in
his first year.

In 1927, Georgia started the
season 9–0. That included a win
over powerhouse Yale. Georgia
became known as the "Dream
and Wonder" team.

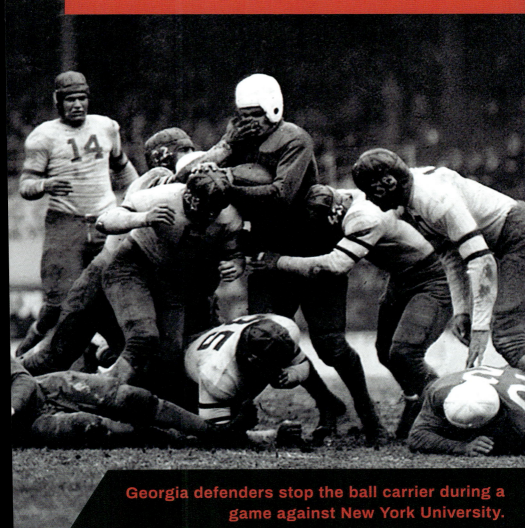

BECOMING THE BULLDOGS

In 1920, a writer described Georgia's football team as bulldogs. He thought it would make a good nickname. Days later, a different writer used the same nickname. Since then, Georgia has been known as the Bulldogs.

Georgia defenders stop the ball carrier during a game against New York University.

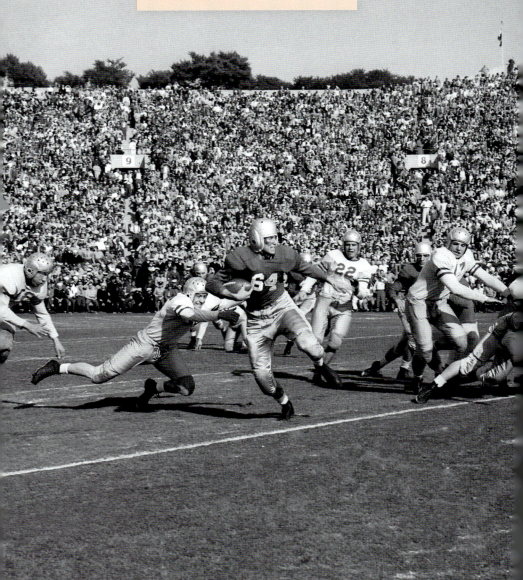

Georgia halfback Lamar Davis (64) runs the ball against UCLA during the Rose Bowl.

Wallace Butts took over as Georgia's coach in 1939. He turned the team into a power. In 1941, the Bulldogs lost only one game. In 1942, Georgia's defense shut out five opponents. The team earned a trip to the Rose Bowl that season. The Bulldogs beat UCLA 9–0.

HISTORIC RIVALRY

Georgia played Auburn for the first time in 1892. The teams have played each other nearly every year since. The game is known as the "Deep South's Oldest Rivalry."

Butts led Georgia to an undefeated season in 1946. He continued coaching the team until 1960. Replacing him wouldn't be easy. Georgia hired Vince Dooley before the 1964 season. He was only 31 years old. And he had never been a head coach. But he proved to be up for the task.

UNKNOWN BEGINNINGS

Georgia and Florida started playing each other in the early 1900s. But neither team agrees when the rivalry began. Their first official meeting happened in 1915. Since 1933, the teams have played at a neutral site. Each game takes place in Jacksonville, Florida.

Under Dooley, Georgia became one of the top teams in the Southeastern Conference (SEC). In 1980, no one could beat the Bulldogs. They went 11–0 that season. They earned a trip to the Sugar Bowl. There they beat Notre Dame 17–10. Georgia was named the national champion!

Players carry Vince Dooley off the field after Georgia's victory over Notre Dame in the Sugar Bowl.

FRANK SINKWICH

Few players were as tough as Frank Sinkwich. The running back broke his jaw early in the 1941 season. But that didn't stop him. He set the SEC single-season rushing record.

Sinkwich played even better in 1942. That year, he set a new SEC passing record. Then he competed in the Rose Bowl with two sprained ankles. He scored Georgia's only touchdown in a 9–0 win. Sinkwich won the Heisman Trophy in 1942. That honor goes to the best player in college football.

SINKWICH EARNED ALL-AMERICA HONORS IN BOTH 1941 AND 1942.

CHAPTER 3

LEGENDS

Vernon Smith couldn't be stopped against Yale in 1929. He scored a touchdown on a blocked punt. Then he kicked the extra point. Later, he caught a touchdown pass. He also recorded a safety. Smith scored all of Georgia's points in a 15–0 win.

Vernon Smith was named to the All-America team in the 1931 season.

Frank Sinkwich was Georgia's star player in the early 1940s. Then in 1945, John Rauch arrived. He earned the starting quarterback job as a freshman. Rauch led the team for four years. He threw for 4,044 yards. At the time, it was a college football record.

WELCOME HOME

Running back Charley Trippi helped the Bulldogs win the Rose Bowl in the 1942 season. He then served in the US military during World War II (1939–1945). Trippi returned to Georgia in 1945. He helped the Bulldogs go undefeated in 1946.

John Rauch
was the first
player to start
in four straight
bowl games.

Fran Tarkenton (10) listens to head coach Wally Butts during a 1959 practice.

Fran Tarkenton grew up in Athens. The quarterback led the local high school to a state title. Then he helped Georgia win the SEC title in 1959.

Offensive linemen had a hard time blocking Bill Stanfill. The defensive tackle made three All-SEC teams.

DROUGHT BREAKER

In 1956, Georgia lost to Georgia Tech for the eighth year in a row. Theron Sapp changed that in 1957. The running back scored the game's only touchdown. Georgia won 7–0. Sapp earned the nickname "Drought Breaker."

Scott Woerner (right) grabs an interception in the Sugar Bowl.

Georgia's 1980 team had two great defensive backs. Scott Woerner intercepted two passes in the Sugar Bowl. Terry Hoage blocked a field-goal attempt in the game. Two years later, Hoage recorded 12 interceptions. That set a single-season school record.

On offense, Herschel Walker led the way. Defenses couldn't stop the speedy running back. In 1980, he led the SEC in rushing yards as a freshman.

HERSCHEL WALKER

Few players were as reliable as Herschel Walker. The running back played at Georgia for three years. He was an All-American all three seasons.

Defenders couldn't catch Walker. He used that speed to rack up 5,259 rushing yards. No player had ever reached that mark in three years. Walker finished as a Heisman finalist in all three of his seasons at Georgia. He won the award in 1982 as a junior.

HERSCHEL WALKER SCORED 52 TOUCHDOWNS DURING HIS THREE SEASONS WITH THE BULLDOGS.

CHAPTER 4

RECENT HISTORY

Vince Dooley stepped down after the 1988 season. He had won 201 games at Georgia. That set a school record. Dooley coached the Bulldogs for 25 years. During that time, they posted only one losing season.

Running back Tim Worley led Georgia to a record of 9–3 in Vince Dooley's final season.

The Bulldogs struggled in the 1990s. Then they hired Mark Richt in 2001. In his second year, Georgia went 13–1. The Bulldogs were always contenders under Richt. He led Georgia to nine bowl wins.

MEETING AGAIN

Before going to Georgia, Mark Richt coached at Florida State. He worked for legendary head coach Bobby Bowden. After the 2002 season, Georgia faced Florida State in the Sugar Bowl. Richt led Georgia to a 26–13 win over Bowden.

Musa Smith ran for 145 yards in Georgia's Sugar Bowl win over Florida State.

Kirby Smart played for Georgia in the 1990s. In 2016, he became the team's head coach. Smart focused on tough defense. In his second season, he led Georgia to the College Football Playoff.

TOUGH LOSS

Georgia reached the national title game in the 2017 season. The Bulldogs led Alabama 13–0 at halftime. Alabama stormed back to force overtime. Georgia kicked a field goal to take the lead. But Alabama scored a touchdown to win.

Georgia's defense smothers the quarterback in a 2017 game against Mississippi State.

Everything came together for the Bulldogs in 2021. They reached the national title game. There they beat Alabama 33–18. The Bulldogs didn't slow down after that. They went 15–0 in 2022. That included a dominant display in the national title game. Georgia pounded Texas Christian University 65–7.

FAMILIAR FOES

Kirby Smart coached at Alabama from 2007 to 2015. He worked under head coach Nick Saban. When Smart went to Georgia, he and Saban faced off six times. Saban beat Smart five times. But Smart's one win came in the national title game.

Georgia players celebrate after winning the national title game in January 2022.

CHAPTER 5

MODERN STARS

Defensive back Champ Bailey did just about everything in 1998. He won the Nagurski Trophy. That's given to the country's best defensive player. On offense, he racked up 828 yards. Bailey also returned punts and kicks.

Champ Bailey (4) recorded more than 1,100 total yards in the 1998 season.

Matthew Stafford topped 7,700 passing yards in his three seasons with Georgia.

Matthew Stafford diced up defenses in 2008. He led the SEC with 3,459 passing yards. Freshman wide receiver A. J. Green was one of his favorite targets. Aaron Murray became Georgia's quarterback in 2010. He started for four years. Murray threw for 13,166 yards. That set a school record.

SACK MACHINE

David Pollack crushed quarterbacks. He was named SEC Defensive Player of the Year in 2002. He won the award again in 2004. Pollack finished his career with 36 sacks. No one in team history has more.

Nick Chubb scores a touchdown in a 2014 game against Auburn.

Todd Gurley took the SEC by storm in 2012. The freshman running back recorded 1,502 total yards. As a junior, he posted 968 total yards in six games. However, an injury cut his season short.

TALENTED DUO

From 2014 to 2017, no team had more talent at running back than Georgia. Nick Chubb ran for 4,769 yards in that span. Sony Michel added 3,638 yards on the ground. Only Herschel Walker has more rushing yards in school history.

Georgia had the nation's best defense in 2021. Defensive tackle Jordan Davis used his huge frame to stop the run. Behind him, linebacker Nakobe Dean covered the entire field.

Quarterback Stetson Bennett led the Bulldogs to two national titles. Many of Bennett's passes went to Brock Bowers. The tight end caught touchdown passes in both national title games.

Jordan Davis celebrates a sack during a 2019 game against Texas A&M.

STETSON BENNETT

No top schools wanted Stetson Bennett. So, he went to Georgia in 2017 as a walk-on. By 2021, he still wasn't the starting quarterback. But he won the job during the season. He ended up helping the Bulldogs win a national title.

Bennett couldn't be stopped in 2022. He was a Heisman finalist that year. In that season's title game, he ran for two touchdowns. And he threw for four more. That tied a record for the most total touchdowns in a national championship game.

STETSON BENNETT LED THE SEC WITH 4,128 PASSING YARDS IN 2022.

CHAPTER 6

TEAM TRIVIA

Georgia is one of the most successful teams in college football history. Going into the 2025 season, the Bulldogs had played in 63 bowl games. Only Alabama had played in more.

Led by Kendall Milton, Georgia thumped Florida State 63–3 in the 2023 Orange Bowl.

Uga and Hairy Dawg pose for a photo before a game against Georgia Tech.

For years, Georgia didn't have a mascot. Before 1920, the team was known as the "Red and Black." Those were the team's jersey colors. In 1956, Uga became Georgia's mascot. Uga is a white English bulldog. Over the years, several dogs have served as Uga.

OTHER MASCOT

Hairy Dawg became a team mascot in 1981. The mascot's costume is a bulldog in a full Georgia football uniform. Hairy Dawg also wears a spiked collar.

The Chapel Bell has been on Georgia's campus since 1832. In 1894, Georgia beat Auburn for the first time. Georgia students wanted to celebrate beating their rival. So, they rang the Chapel Bell. Today, students still ring the bell after wins.

SILVER PANTS

Georgia players began wearing silver pants in 1939. But in 1964, Vince Dooley decided to start using white pants. Dooley brought back the silver pants in 1980. The Bulldogs won a national title that year. Georgia has kept the silver pants ever since.

Georgia has been using its famous "G" logo since 1964.

Fans go wild as Georgia players make their way toward Sanford Stadium.

In 2001, Mark Richt started the Dawg Walk. Before each home game, Georgia players walk from the team bus to the stadium. Hundreds of fans cheer for the players. The marching band plays "Glory, Glory to Old Georgia."

RETIRED NUMBERS

Many great athletes have played for Georgia. But the team has retired only four numbers. Theron Sapp, Frank Sinkwich, Charley Trippi, and Herschel Walker are the only players who earned that honor.

TEAM RECORDS

All-Time Passing Yards: 13,166
Aaron Murray (2010–13)

All-Time Rushing Yards: 5,259
Herschel Walker (1980–82)

All-Time Receiving Yards: 3,093
Terrence Edwards (1999–2002)

All-Time Touchdowns: 52
Herschel Walker (1980–82)

All-Time Scoring: 440
Rodrigo Blankenship (2016–19)

All-Time Interceptions: 16
Jake Scott (1967–68), Bacarri Rambo (2009–12), Dominick Sanders (2014–17)

All-Time Sacks: 36
David Pollack (2001–04)

All-Time Coaching Wins: 201
Vince Dooley (1964–88)

Heisman Trophy Winners: 2
Frank Sinkwich (1942), Herschel Walker (1982)

National Championships: 4
1942†, 1980, 2021, 2022

† Season in which more than one school claims the national title.

All statistics are accurate through 2024.

TIMELINE

 1892

 1920

1942

1964

1980

Georgia plays its first football game.

Frank Sinkwich becomes the first Georgia player to win the Heisman Trophy.

Dooley leads the Bulldogs to a national championship.

Herman Stegeman leads Georgia to an undefeated season.

Vince Dooley begins his first season as Georgia's head coach.

1982

2001

2017

2021

2022

Mark Richt begins his first season as head coach.

Behind a great defense, Georgia wins the national championship.

Herschel Walker wins the Heisman Trophy.

In his second season, Kirby Smart leads Georgia to the national title game.

Stetson Bennett leads the Bulldogs to back-to-back national titles.

COMPREHENSION QUESTIONS

Write your answers on a separate piece of paper.

1. Write a paragraph that explains the main ideas of Chapter 4.

2. Who do you think was the greatest player in Georgia history? Why?

3. Which player won the Nagurski Trophy in 1998?
   A. Herschel Walker
   B. Champ Bailey
   C. David Pollack

4. Why did Theron Sapp earn the nickname "Drought Breaker"?
   A. He ended Georgia's losing streak against Georgia Tech.
   B. He scored the most touchdowns in Georgia history.
   C. He left the Georgia Bulldogs to serve in the military.

5. What does **contenders** mean in this book?

*The Bulldogs were always **contenders** under Richt. He led Georgia to nine bowl wins.*

    A. teams that only play schools from the Deep South

    B. teams that don't play well during the regular season

    C. teams that have a good chance of winning a title

6. What does **dominant** mean in this book?

*They went 15–0 in 2022. That included a **dominant** display in the national title game. Georgia pounded Texas Christian University 65–7.*

    A. unable to run the ball well

    B. much better than other teams

    C. having more losses than wins

Answer key on page 64.

GLOSSARY

conference
A group of teams that make up part of a sports league.

freshman
A student in their first year of college.

intercepted
Caught an opponent's pass as a defensive player.

mascot
A figure that is the symbol of a sports team.

neutral
Not supporting either side.

overtime
An extra period that happens if two teams are tied at the end of the fourth quarter.

rivalry
An ongoing competition that brings out strong emotion from fans and players.

sacks
Plays that happen when a defender tackles the quarterback before he can throw the ball.

safety
A play in which a defensive player tackles an opponent in their own end zone. The defensive team earns two points.

shut out
Did not allow the opponent to score.

walk-on
A player without a scholarship.

TO LEARN MORE

BOOKS

Lowe, Alexander. *G.O.A.T. Football Running Backs*. Lerner Publications, 2023.

Scheff, Matt. *Matthew Stafford: Football Star*. Focus Readers, 2023.

Streeter, Anthony. *College Football Championship All-Time Greats*. Press Box Books, 2025.

ONLINE RESOURCES

Visit **www.apexeditions.com** to find links and resources related to this title.

ABOUT THE AUTHOR

Luke Hanlon is a sportswriter and editor based in Minneapolis. He's written dozens of nonfiction sports books for kids and spends a lot of his free time watching his favorite Minnesota sports teams.

INDEX

ANSWER KEY:
1. Answers will vary; 2. Answers will vary; 3. B; 4. A; 5. C; 6.

City Trucks

Julie Murray

Abdo Kids Junior
is an Imprint of Abdo Kids
abdobooks.com

Abdo
TRUCKS AT WORK
Kids

abdobooks.com

Published by Abdo Kids, a division of ABDO, P.O. Box 398166, Minneapolis, Minnesota 55439.
Copyright © 2024 by Abdo Consulting Group, Inc. International copyrights reserved in all countries.
No part of this book may be reproduced in any form without written permission from the publisher.
Abdo Kids Junior™ is a trademark and logo of Abdo Kids.

Printed in the United States of America, North Mankato, Minnesota.

052023

092023

THIS BOOK CONTAINS
RECYCLED MATERIALS

Photo Credits: Alamy, Getty Images, Shutterstock

Production Contributors: Teddy Borth, Jennie Forsberg, Grace Hansen

Design Contributors: Candice Keimig, Pakou Moua

Library of Congress Control Number: 2022946714

Publisher's Cataloging-in-Publication Data

Names: Murray, Julie, author.

Title: City trucks / by Julie Murray

Description: Minneapolis, Minnesota : Abdo Kids, 2024 | Series: Trucks at work | Includes online resources
    and index.

Identifiers: ISBN 9781098266110 (lib. bdg.) | ISBN 9781098266813 (ebook) | ISBN 9781098267162
    (Read-to-me ebook)

Subjects: LCSH: Trucks--Juvenile literature. | Vehicles--Juvenile literature. | City transit--Juvenile
    literature.

Classification: DDC 388.32--dc23

Table of Contents

City Trucks

City trucks help keep cities running smoothly!

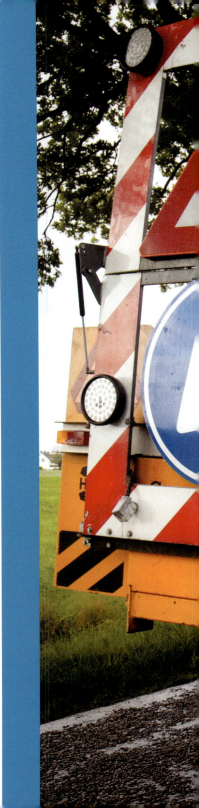

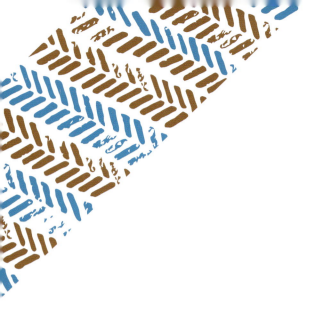

A mail truck brings the mail.

A mail carrier drives it.

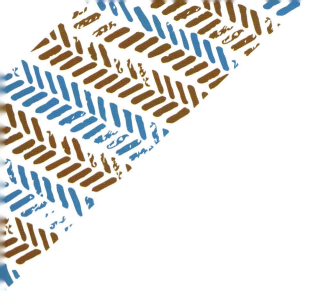

A garbage truck is big!

The arm lifts the can.

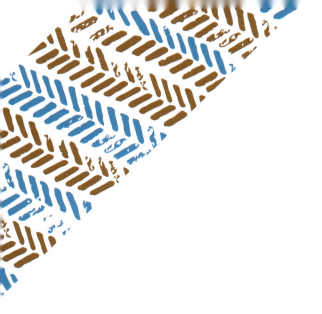

Al drives a water truck. He waters the street flowers.

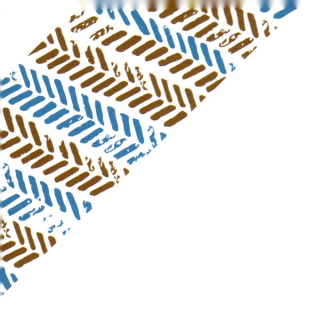

A **recycling** truck comes
to Val's house once a week.

A bucket truck lifts Ian.

He fixes the power line.

HEIGHT
10FT.-8IN.

15

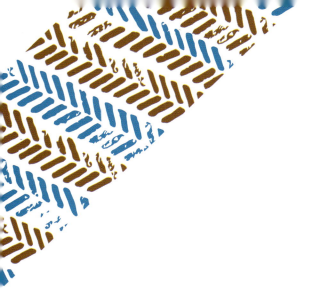

Pam drives a snowplow.

She makes the roads safe.

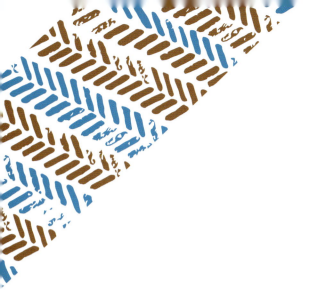

A **freight** truck moves goods. Sam helps unload.

What trucks do you see

in your city?

More City Trucks

deicing truck

street cleaner

striping truck

tow truck

Glossary

freight
goods shipped by boat, plane, train, or truck.

recycling
the activity of processing things so that they can be used again.

Index

Abdo Kids ONLINE
FREE! ONLINE MULTIMEDIA RESOURCES

Visit **abdokids.com** to access crafts, games, videos, and more!

Use Abdo Kids code

TCK6110

or scan this QR code!